THE TEAM LEADERSHIP PRACTICES INVENTORY [TEAM LPI]

Measuring Leadership of Teams

Participant's Workbook

THE TEAM LEADERSHIP PRACTICES INVENTORY [TEAM LPI]

Measuring Leadership of Teams

Participant's Workbook

James M. Kouzes

Barry Z. Posner, Ph.D.

JOSSEY-BASS/PFEIFFER
A Wiley Company
www.pfeiffer.com

Published by

JOSSEY-BASS/PFEIFFER
A Wiley Company
989 Market Street
San Francisco, CA 94103-1741
415.433.1740; Fax 415.433.0499
800.274.4434; Fax 800.569.0443

| www.pfeiffer.com |

Jossey-Bass/Pfeiffer is a registered trademark of John Wiley & Sons, Inc.

ISBN:0-7879-3906-4

Printed in the United States of America

Printing 10 9 8 7 6

We at Jossey-Bass strive to use the most environmentally sensitive paper stocks available to us. Our publications are printed on acid-free recycled stock whenever possible, and our paper always meets or exceeds minimum GPO and EPA requirements.

CONTENTS

The TEAM LPI and the Practices of Exemplary Leadership

The Team Leadership Practices Inventory (TEAM LPI) focuses on the key behaviors and actions of high-performing teams and self-directed work groups. It is useful as a guide in beginning team-development activities and as feedback in ongoing improvements efforts. The "team" can be members of a functional group, an interdisciplinary project team, a task force, or a matrix group of either permanent or temporary status.

The TEAM LPI also may be used by a manager or leader with his or her work team to explore and discuss how well the fundamental leadership functions are being fulfilled within the team. The basic premise of the TEAM LPI is that the leadership responsibilities do not reside exclusively with the formal manager or leader; in high-performing work groups everyone is a leader. In fact, one of the formal leader's fundamental tasks is to liberate the leader in each team member—to turn each member into a leader.

The TEAM LPI is based on the Kouzes-Posner Leadership Model, as described in the book *The Leadership Challenge: How to Keep Getting Extraordinary Things Done in Organizations.*[1] According to Kouzes and Posner's research studies, when people are at their personal best as leaders they are engaged in five key leadership practices: challenging the process, inspiring a shared vision, enabling others to act, modeling the way, and encouraging the heart. Subsequent research applying this model to work groups demonstrated that these same leadership practices are common among members of high-performing teams. The TEAM LPI helps you to discover to what extent your team uses these five practices:

- *Challenging the Process* entails being willing to take risks, exploring new alternatives, experimenting, learning from mistakes, and supporting one another in these efforts.

- *Inspiring a Shared Vision* means developing a common understanding of what the team is trying to accomplish, realizing how the team's efforts are aligned with larger organizational goals, and using values to guide future actions.

---

[1]*The Leadership Challenge: How to Keep Getting Extraordinary Things Done in Organizations* by James M. Kouzes and Barry Z. Posner, 1995, San Francisco: Jossey-Bass. This book may be purchased from Jossey-Bass/Pfeiffer, 989 Market Street, San Francisco, CA 94103, phone 800-274-4434 or FAX 800-569-0433.

I

- *Enabling Others to Act* involves assuming an active role in setting goals and planning projects, establishing cooperative objectives, sharing information and keeping one another informed, and demonstrating mutual respect for one another's ideas and competencies.

- *Modeling the Way* means translating shared values into actions and deeds, being accountable to one another, influencing by example, and breaking projects down into achievable steps so that small "wins" can be accomplished along the way.

- *Encouraging the Heart* entails feeling emotionally connected to the team, providing timely feedback, pointing with pride to team accomplishments, and celebrating together the achievement of milestones.

The original Leadership Practices Inventory (LPI)[2] was developed to provide individual feedback and assessment concerning a leader's use of these five practices. The LPI comes in a Self version, which is completed by a leader, and in an Observer version, which is completed by a leader's constituents (direct reports and, if desired, manager, coworkers, and customers/suppliers/etc.).

Preliminary research and data analyses reveal that the Kouzes-Posner Leadership Model can be extended and applied to work groups, project teams, and task forces as well as to individual managers or leaders. This is especially true for self-directed work groups and teams.

The TEAM LPI is designed to be self-scored by the team members. This scoring system allows maximum flexibility and offers team members the chance to develop ownership of the inventory data as well as a firsthand sense of the range of differences and similarities in their common experiences. As both a work group and as individuals, team members can identify leadership practices and behaviors that need development and support. The team can learn about the culture of leadership and the key performance and behavior norms that govern their work lives.

---

[2] *The Leadership Practices Inventory (LPI)*, 2nd ed., by James M. Kouzes and Barry Z. Posner, 1997, San Francisco: Pfeiffer. This instrument is available from Jossey-Bass/Pfeiffer.

Recording Scores, Reviewing Results, & Planning Action

There are a number of ways to examine the results of the TEAM LPI, but the most effective approach is to meet with the other members of your team to discuss and analyze scores and to plan action based on the feedback. The following ten-step process is recommended:

1. Post a newsprint sheet for each of the five key leadership practices and label them accordingly (that is, Challenging the Process, Inspiring a Shared Vision, Enabling Others to Act, Modeling the Way, and Encouraging the Heart).

2. On each newsprint poster, prepare a grid for recording team members' scores. Each grid is similar to the ones provided in this workbook, with the following changes and additions (see the sample newsprint grid in Figure 1):

• Omit the "Self" column.

• List the item numbers vertically to the left of the grids, also list brief versions of the summary statements that appear next to the item numbers in the workbook.

Practices		Karen	Jack	Chris	Terry	Dale	Pat
1. Seek challenges							
6. Stay up-to-date							
11. Challenge status quo							
16. Innovate							
21. "What can we learn?"							
26. Take risks							
TOTALS							
Grand Total _____		**Team Average** _____					

Figure 1. Sample of Newsprint Grid for Challenging the Process

3

- List the names or initials of all team members horizontally at the top of the grid (one vertical column per member).

- Draw horizontal lines to separate the item numbers and vertical lines to separate the members' names or initials.

3. Each team member refers to page 4 of his or her completed TEAM LPI. Under the heading "Transferring Ratings" are five vertical columns of scores. Each of these columns represents one of the five key leadership practices: The first column on the left lists ratings for Challenging the Process; the second column lists ratings for Inspiring a Shared Vision; the third, Enabling Others to Act; and so on. The team members record their own scores (1) in their workbooks and (2) on the newsprint posters, under their names or initials. After all scores have been recorded on posters, each member records names/initials and the other members' scores in his or her workbook.

4. On each newsprint poster, write "Totals" under the last item number, and draw a row of boxes at the bottom of the grid. For each key leadership practice, total the vertical columns separately and write the totals in the boxes in the row marked "Totals." Then add together all of the totals for all members; record this number under the grid structure; and write "Grand Total" next to the number. To obtain the average team-member score, divide the grand total by the number of team members who completed the TEAM LPI; then write this average on the newsprint, with the words "Team Average" next to it. After all totals and averages have been recorded on posters, each team member copies them into his or her workbook. In addition, each member calculates and records his or her own average rating for each key leadership practice.

5. For each inventory item on each poster, circle the numbers that represent the highest and lowest scores. After all scores have been circled on posters, each team member circles the same scores in his or her workbook. This circling procedure illustrates the range of differences in perception of behaviors among team members.

6. Each member of the team works independently to make notes about the questions following the grids for each leadership practice (pages 6 through 15 in this workbook). Each member's notes should include a personal assessment of what he or she and the other members can do to make the team more effective at using each leadership practice.

7. The members discuss the leadership practices one by one, concentrating on the implications of the feedback and sharing the contents of the notes made in the previous step. Here are some issues that the team should address for each practice:

- How do you account for the frequency indicated in the team average?

- Where do individual perceptions agree? Where do they disagree? How can discrepancies in perception be explained?

- What forces *drive* your team to engage in this practice? What forces *restrain* your team? Consider behaviors (such as actions, strategies, and techniques) as well as routines, systems, and structures.

- How can the team members who feel comfortable with this practice help those who do not? What can your team do to support the behaviors involved in this practice? What will you personally do?

  Highlights of this discussion are recorded on newsprint and posted.

8. After reviewing each of the five leadership practices as outlined in the previous step, the team should take a short break.

9. The team members choose one to three key leadership practices in which they, as a team, would like to improve. Then the team completes the process described in the Action Planning Work Sheet for each key leadership practice chosen, determining the appropriate action steps for leadership development. Plans are recorded on newsprint and posted.[3]

10. The members decide how the team will evaluate progress in taking the necessary steps to meet the goals posted on newsprint. Then the team discusses and completes the Keeping Commitments Work Sheet on page 22. All plans are recorded on newsprint. All team members should retain copies of the plans: Either they may copy plans into their workbooks, or after the workshop one team member may collect the newsprint plans, reproduce them in handout form, and then distribute the handout to all members.

---

[3]This workbook includes three copies of the Action Planning Work Sheet (pages 16 through 21). Each work sheet provides plenty of space for jotting down notes about the team's plans for taking action. The Keeping Commitments Work Sheet referred to in the next step also offers space for making notes.

Challenging the Process

Record scores in accordance with the instructions that begin on page 3. As you look at individual scores, remember the rating system that was used:

1 means that the members of your work team *rarely or very seldom* do what is described in the statement.

2 means that the members of your work team do what is described *once in a while*.

3 means that the members of your work team *sometimes* do what is described.

4 means that the members of your work team *fairly often* do what is described.

5 means that the members of your work team *very frequently or almost always* do what is described in the statement.

	Self	Other Members										
1. Seek challenges												
6. Stay up-to-date												
11. Challenge status quo												
16. Look for ways to innovate												
21. Ask "What can we learn?"												
26. Experiment and take risks												
TOTALS												

Grand Total_____

Self Average_____   **Team Average**_____

According to this feedback, how is your team doing on *Challenging the Process?*

What does your team need to do to become even more effective at *Challenging the Process?*

Start:

Stop:

Continue:

Inspiring a Shared Vision

Record scores in accordance with the instructions that begin on page 3. As you look at individual scores, remember the rating system that was used:

1 means that the members of your work team *rarely or very seldom* do what is described in the statement.

2 means that the members of your work team do what is described *once in a while*.

3 means that the members of your work team *sometimes* do what is described.

4 means that the members of your work team *fairly often* do what is described.

5 means that the members of your work team *very frequently or almost always* do what is described in the statement.

	Self	Other Members									
2. Describe future we can create											
7. Share future dreams											
12. Communicate positive outlook											
17. Enlist in a common vision											
22. Forecast the future											
27. Contagiously excited about future											
TOTALS											

Grand Total_____

Self Average_____   **Team Average**_____

According to this feedback, how is your team doing on *Inspiring a Shared Vision?*

What does your team need to do to become even more effective at *Inspiring a Shared Vision?*

Start:

Stop:

Continue:

Enabling Others to Act

Record scores in accordance with the instructions that begin on page 3. As you look at individual scores, remember the rating system that was used:

1 means that the members of your work team *rarely or very seldom* do what is described in the statement.

2 means that the members of your work team do what is described *once in a while*.

3 means that the members of your work team *sometimes* do what is described.

4 means that the members of your work team *fairly often* do what is described.

5 means that the members of your work team *very frequently or almost always* do what is described in the statement.

	Self	Other Members									
3. Involve others in planning											
8. Treat others with respect											
13. Allow others to make decisions											
18. Develop cooperative relationships											
23. Create atmosphere of trust											
28. Get others to own project											
TOTALS											

Grand Total_____

Self Average_____   **Team Average**_____

According to this feedback, how is your team doing on *Enabling Others to Act?*

What does your team need to do to become even more effective at *Enabling Others to Act?*

    Start:

    Stop:

    Continue:

Modeling the Way

Record scores in accordance with the instructions that begin on page 3. As you look at individual scores, remember the rating system that was used:

1 means that the members of your work team *rarely or very seldom* do what is described in the statement.

2 means that the members of your work team do what is described *once in a while*.

3 means that the members of your work team *sometimes* do what is described.

4 means that the members of your work team *fairly often* do what is described.

5 means that the members of your work team *very frequently or almost always* do what is described in the statement.

	Self	Other Members									
4. Clear on leadership philosophy											
9. Break projects into steps											
14. Ensure values are adhered to											
19. Let others know beliefs/values											
24. Practice what is espoused											
29. Set clear goals and milestones											
TOTALS											

Grand Total_____

Self Average_____   **Team Average**_____

According to this feedback, how is your team doing on *Modeling the Way?*

What does your team need to do to become even more effective at *Modeling the Way?*

Start:

Stop:

Continue:

Encouraging the Heart

Record scores in accordance with the instructions that begin on page 3. As you look at individual scores, remember the rating system that was used:

1 means that the members of your work team *rarely or very seldom* do what is described in the statement.

2 means that the members of your work team do what is described *once in a while.*

3 means that the members of your work team *sometimes* do what is described.

4 means that the members of your work team *fairly often* do what is described.

5 means that the members of your work team *very frequently or almost always* do what is described in the statement.

	Self	Other Members									
5. Celebrate milestones											
10. Recognize others' contributions											
15. Give praise for job well done											
20. Give team appreciation/support											
25. Find ways to celebrate											
30. Tell others about team's work											
TOTALS											

Grand Total_____

Self Average_____   **Team Average**_____

According to this feedback, how is your team doing on *Encouraging the Heart*?

What does your team need to do to become even more effective at *Encouraging the Heart?*

Start:

Stop:

Continue:

Action Planning Work Sheet

After discussing the data from the TEAM LPI, the next step for you and your fellow team members is to decide what actions the team will take to become more effective at using the key leadership practices. Complete the following action-planning steps. *Note: Three Action Planning Work Sheets are included in this guidebook; use one form for each leadership practice that the team plans to improve.*

The leadership practice that the team wants to improve:

_____

1. What *specifically* would you and your fellow team members like to be better able to do? Here is an example: We would like to celebrate more of our accomplishments.

2. What specific actions could you and your fellow team members take? What options do you have? (Do not censor any ideas at this point; generate as many as you can, regardless of how workable they are.)

3. What actions *will* you and your fellow team members take to meet your improvement goal? (Select from your list of options in the previous step.)

4. What is the *first* action you and your fellow team members will take to improve your leadership skills? Who will be involved? When will you begin?

Action   **People Involved**   **Target Date**

5. Complete this sentence: "We will know we have improved as a team when . . ."

6. On what date do you and your fellow team members plan to review your progress?

Action Planning Work Sheet

After discussing the data from the TEAM LPI, the next step for you and your fellow team members is to decide what actions the team will take to become more effective at using the key leadership practices. Complete the following action-planning steps. *Note: Three Action Planning Work Sheets are included in this guidebook; use one form for each leadership that the team plans to improve.*

The leadership practice that the team wants to improve:

_____

1. What *specifically* would you and your fellow team members like to be better able to do? Here is an example: We would like to celebrate more of our accomplishments.

2. What specific actions could you and your fellow team members take? What options do you have? (Do not censor any ideas at this point; generate as many as you can, regardless of how workable they are.)

3. What actions *will* you and your fellow team members take to meet your improvement goal? (Select from your list of options in the previous step.)

4. What is the *first* action you and your fellow team members will take to improve your leadership skills? Who will be involved? When will you begin?

Action	People Involved	Target Date

5. Complete this sentence: "We will know we have improved as a team when . . ."

6. On what date do you and your fellow team members plan to review your progress?

Action Planning Work Sheet

After discussing the data from the TEAM LPI, the next step for you and your fellow team members is to decide what actions the team will take to become more effective at using the key leadership practices. Complete the following action-planning steps. *Note: Three Action Planning Work Sheets are included in this guidebook; use one form for each leadership that the team plans to improve.*

The leadership practice that the team wants to improve:

_____

1. What *specifically* would you and your fellow team members like to be better able to do? Here is an example: We would like to celebrate more of our accomplishments.

2. What specific actions could you and your fellow team members take? What options do you have? (Do not censor any ideas at this point; generate as many as you can, regardless of how workable they are.)

3. What actions *will* you and your fellow team members take to meet your improvement goal? (Select from your list of options in the previous step.)

4. What is the *first* action you and your fellow team members will take to improve your leadership skills? Who will be involved? When will you begin?

Action	People Involved	Target Date

5. Complete this sentence: "We will know we have improved as a team when . . ."

6. On what date do you and your fellow team members plan to review your progress?

_____

Keeping Commitments Work Sheet

It is not always easy for a team to develop its leadership effectiveness. You and your fellow team members will need to help and support one another. By answering the following questions, you and the other team members can make plans about how to keep yourselves focused on meeting the team's commitments:

What is at least one way that you and your fellow team members can *keep yourselves motivated* if you get bogged down, sidetracked, or discouraged?

Whom can you and your fellow team members count on for *help and support* when you need it?

What can you and your fellow team members do to *reward yourselves* for keeping the commitments you have made?

Possible Next Steps

Here are some follow-up steps that you and your fellow team members might want to take:

1. Make a team-leadership contract. Given the TEAM LPI feedback and a shared commitment to developing leadership effectiveness within the team, you and your fellow members can meet to consider any additional changes that make sense. During this meeting state what you personally are willing and able to do as well as what help you need from your fellow team members. (Because team leadership involves interaction among members, any changes you make in your own behavior may necessitate changes in the behavior of one or more of your fellow team members.) You and your fellow team members should discuss and agree on what behavioral changes will be made, how you will know that changes have been made, and whether those changes have made a difference.

2. Collect follow-up data. Seriously consider completing the TEAM LPI again in three to six months and periodically thereafter to determine how much change in leadership practices has occurred and in which areas further changes might be warranted. Continuing to collect data signals the team members' collective commitment to leadership development. As you and your fellow team members become accustomed to the Kouzes-Posner Leadership Model, a common language can emerge as well as shared norms of behavior and responsibility.

3. Conduct an "upward" leadership appraisal. Your team might want to complete the Observer version of the original LPI to assess the formal manager's use of the five key leadership practices. (The manager would complete the Self version.) After the Self and Observer forms have been completed, you and your fellow team members meet with the manager to discuss the effectiveness and appropriateness of the manager's leadership. Together you identify not only obstacles that hinder team performance but also behaviors and practices that promote and sustain your team's effectiveness.

4. Have each team member complete the LPI-Self to assess his or her individual leadership practices and behaviors. Data from other people, including some fellow team members as well as other colleagues outside your immediate work group, can be collected with the LPI-Observer. This feedback may help each individual to understand more about his or her own particular leadership strengths and areas for personal development.

5. Have the entire team watch *The Leadership Challenge* videocassette.[4] This videocassette provides an overview of the Kouzes-Posner Leadership Model and presents four case studies illustrating the leadership practices in action. You and your fellow team members also might want to watch *Leadership in Action.* This videocassette looks at the "personal-best leadership experience" of one manager at DuPont. The story, told by the manager himself and by others involved, illustrates how this manager used the five key leadership practices to accomplish an extraordinary task.

6. Have nonmembers complete the TEAM LPI to evaluate your team. These people, who may be suppliers, customers, partners, or members of another unit or department, can provide you with further insight into how your team's behaviors, actions, and leadership effectiveness are perceived. If the nonmembers are people with whom the team has to interact regularly, the data that emerge may open avenues for mutual cooperation and intergroup problem solving.

---

[4]*The Leadership Challenge,* a twenty-six minute VHS videocassette is available from Jossey-Bass/Pfeiffer.

Notes

Notes